CRAIL 1889

by

ERIC EUNSON

Cover illustration: Shoregate from High Street, July 1889.

Published by Stenlake & McCourt, 1 Overdale Street,
Langside, Glasgow, G42 9PZ.
Tel: 041 632 2304

INTRODUCTION

In 1889, Crail was just beginning to recover from a century of decline. The small harbour brought the town prosperity through Dutch and other European trade in the sixteenth century. In the eighteenth century, Crail was a major port for visiting herring-boats from Angus and the Mearns. In the 1790's, the port went into decline not because of over-fishing, but because the herring no longer visited the Forth due to a change in migration patterns. When the herring returned and the Forth fishing recovered in the 1830's, Crail harbour had been outmoded by the larger and improved harbours of the neighbouring villages. As a result, Crail gained little from the upturn, although local fishermen continued to land large quantities of crabs and lobsters.

In 1886, the railway was extended from Anstruther to Crail. The following year it reached St. Andrews. After centuries of isolation by land, Crail suddenly became accessible to travellers. Before long, artists and historians discovered the ancient burgh. Soon, Victorian tourists were flocking to Crail in pursuit of the then new fashion for sea bathing. By the end of the decade, long lists of visitors appeared each summer in the local press.

Hutcheson was not the first to photograph Crail, but his pictures are the oldest known comprehensive record of the town. A century on, many of his views are remarkably unchanged. What is notable is a striking air of dereliction and decay. A public water supply had been introduced ten years before, but many homes were still without sanitation. Many other buildings were in a ruinous condition. Fifteen years on in the mid-1900's, Crail had become a popular place for photographers. Many hundreds of views were on sale as picture postcards. By this time, crumbling cottages had been replaced by handsome villas and other properties repaired reflecting the new prosperity brought by tourism.

Eric Eunson June 1989

Caiplie Caves from West. These caves were probably inhabited in prehistoric times. The earliest evidence of human habitation is the large number of Christian crosses incised in the walls. The earliest of these date from the ninth century. Opinions are divided as to whether these were left by followers of the Hungarian missionary St. Adrian who is said to have visited Fife at this time.

Caiplie Caves from the shore showing the entrance to the Chapel Cave on the right. In 1841, excavations in and around this cave unearthed five graves without coffins and a large midden of stones and animal bones. Signs that the cave had been enlarged and parity paved by man were evident. When this picture was taken the caves were being used as a shelter for cattle.

Salmon fishing was carried out both here at Caiplie and at Roome Bay. Salmon was seldom eaten locally and it was considered bad luck to mention it by name at sea. Most of the salmon from Crail was sent to the London market. This photograph shows the salmon fishers' cottages.

This is a view of Crail from the Anstruther road. On the left is the former West United Free Church, now Holy Trinity. The trees have gone, but all the old buildings remain.

These cottages remain at West Braes to this day, although much newer housing has been added to the scene. The two boys sitting on the wall are George and James Ballardie, John Hutcheson's nephews.

The same cottages at West Braes but looking West. The harbour beacon is one of a pair. The other stands near the corner of Temple Crescent. Now electrified, they indicate the passage through the treacherous rocks at the harbour mouth.

The origins of Crail Harbour are uncertain but Dutch influence is probable. Parts of it may date from 1500. The West Pier was designed in 1826 by the engineer Robert Stevenson. It is the smallest of the harbours in the East Neuk being only three quarters of an acre in extent. It cannot admit vessels of more than ten foot draught even at high water.

In the foreground on the left are the old gasworks, long demolished. The wall behind still stands and the holes where the roof beams rested are visible. A useful by-product of coal gas manufacture was pitch which was used extensively on local fishing vessels.

A pleasant scene by the west slip, adjacent to the old gasworks building.

In the centre of the picture is one of the earliest steam fishing boats in the district. The other boats are of the Fifie design with straight bow and stern. The smaller boats of this type were known as "baldies".

In 1881, there were fifty fishermen in Crail, and thirty-four boats. Half of the Crail fleet can be seen here. Due to a shortage of berths, the boats were often hauled onto the harbour wall when not in use. This also provided an opportunity to carry out essential maintenance.

This is the outer wall of the West Pier. Additional mooring space was available here in good weather.

The Castle Walk and the King's Mill form the backdrop for this "baldie" laden with creels, returning from lobster fishing. Baldies derived their name from the Italian revolutionary Garibaldi. Lobsters and partans (edible crabs) are still landed at Crail today.

The building behind the clutter of fishing boats in the foreground is the old Harbour Office which lost its harling when it was restored in the 1960's.

A typical summer afternoon in July 1889. A lady is painting in the Kingsgate, attracting attention from curious children.

From the shore, a view of the eastern slip and back of Shoregate. The stone sea walls were replaced by concrete and brick early this century. The lean-to's have been removed and the house second from right extended.

Modern bungalows now occupy the fields on the skyline. However, a hundred years have scarcely altered the Shoregate. Only the lamp bracket has gone.

Further up the Shoregate there stands Rock House. Behind the children, a ship's figurehead can just be seen. The figurehead almost certainly was from one of the many ships wrecked off Fife Ness. The author has been unable to ascertain its identity or fate.

These 17th century cottages known as Rock Head were demolished early this century when Castle Terrace was built on this site.

Another view of the cottage at Rock Head, with Rock House partly visible to the right.

In July 1889 Crail High Street was rough and unsurfaced.

In the middle distance on the left the way into a small yard can be seen (adjacent to the lamp standard). The post office was built on this site.

Contemporary with the construction of the post office, the three storey tenement building (centre) was extended. The long crow-stepped gable at its rear was lost.

Another lady artist is working at the corner of St. Andrews Road opposite the Golf Hotel. This 18th century coaching inn exhibits a fine example of a corbelled (i.e. inclined) corner.

A view looking down Rose Wynd from High Street. Most of these cottages have been restored, extended, or both. The second forestair has disappeared.

Looking up Rose Wynd. The houses in the foreground have been rebuilt and the forestair has been patched up with brick.

These dilapidated buildings in Tolbooth Wynd were pulled down soon after this picture was taken and replaced by Balfour House. The stone inscribed "GODS BLESSING IS MY LAND AND RENT" was taken from the house in the foreground and incorporated in the new building.

James Peattie, Provost from 1878, was responsible for the planting of trees in the Marketgate. All but four have subsequently been replanted. The tolbooth is in Dutch style and dates from the 17th century.

The shaft of the market cross also dates from the 17th century. The steps are in traditional style but much later. It was re-sited at this location in 1887.

Looking west down Marketgate, this scene is almost unchanged. In 1889, these substantial houses were new. The third on the right is still under construction.

A view of the south side of the Marketgate. Again, essentially unchanged with the exception of the Jubilee Fountain which was added in 1896.

This is possibly the only known photograph of Crail school, demolished in 1890. To the left of the school is the "Blue Stane". According to local legend, it was hurled from the Isle of May at Crail church by the devil. It was a custom for natives of the town to kiss the stone prior to a journey as a pledge that they would return.

St. Mary's Church was probably founded in the 12th century. In common with many other churches in Fife it was consecrated in 1243 by Bishop David De Bernham. Its fine collection of silver, brass, vestments, and books is recorded in its Chatulary (essentially an inventory).

The treasures did not survive the fervour and unrest stirred up among the congregation by John Knox when he preached here in 1559. Little of the original building remains and the whole structure was much altered in 1796 and 1815.

Crail churchyard contains many tombs of exceptional interest. This tomb houses the graves of John Antone Lindsay and his wife John Amelia Antone both of whom died in 1872. The tomb itself though is of a much earlier date.

"Here lyes interred before this tomb
The corpse of Bailie Thomas Young
Aye honest man of good renown
Three times a Bailie in this town
He sixteen years Convener was
But now in the dust he lyes
The 20 of October Born was he
In anno 1683
And died December 6 interrd eight
In anno 1758
So he with great Composure left this stage
In the 76th year of his age
Isobel Martin his Spouse doth lye here
Also six of their children dear."

This castellated vault was "Erected for securing the dead" in 1826. Bodies were stored here to prevent their being stolen by the resurrectionists (grave-robbers). Corpses remained here for six weeks in summer and three months in winter before burial!

This peaceful image shows a view of the east end of Marketgate. Victorian houses now occupy the vegetable plot (left foreground).

An enchanting study of the Nethergate looking eastwards. The building on the left housed the public library.

A contrasting scene, also of the Nethergate, this time looking west. In the foreground tumbledown hovels sit uneasily beside the recently built villas of Downie Terrace.

The King's Mill stood at the back of Nethergate. It was in a ruinous condition when it was demolished in the 1920's. The site was subsequently occupied by a builder's yard which was in turn recently removed.

The exact location of the mill is clear from this angle as the watch house is still extant at the corner of Castle Walk.

Crail from the East showing the 16th century "priory" dovecot. To the left, the front of Downie Terrace.

Roome Bay on a sunny day in July 1889. This was Crail's mediaeval harbour. In the 19th century it was proposed as being an ideal site for a replacement for the existing harbour.

This suggestion was never adopted, and the bay was only used by salmon fishers whose flat-bottomed cobles were easily beached here.